What People sa

A Butterfly Takes ... ...
examples of God's masterful creation, reminding
you of His love and care. Norene Gion has learned
to listen to God and trusted Him to meet her every
need. Her words will inspire you that God finds
delight in you, and He will be your friend, protector,
and provider. Grab a cup of coffee and let God
speak to you through the pages of her book as you
find hope and strength in your walk with God!

Karen Bowling
Executive Director
Nebraska Family Alliance
nebraskafamilyalliance.org

A Butterfly Takes Flight is a delightful walk with
my friend Norene Gion in her journey with the
Lord. Norene helps us see the world through her
eyes and through the lens that God gave her. Her
wisdom and insight from the Holy Spirit are fun and
life-giving. I know you will enjoy the journey and
be blessed that you took a chance on this little
book!

Shawn Lohry
Yasha Ministries
www.yashaministry.org

A Butterfly Takes Flight is a wonderful book about how God speaks to those who walk with the Lord in a close relationship. The Lord reveals spiritual insights if we humble ourselves, listen and pray for revelation knowledge. Ezekiel heard from the Lord, not from the whirlwind that had four creatures, but when he fell on his face the spirit entered him and he heard a clear message from the Lord as the Spirit revealed His glory to him. We can receive also when we meditate on the natural things that lead to spiritual knowledge. I recommend this book written by Norene Gion who has spent time in prayer and meditation in the Holy Spirit. I pray this book will lead others to seek the spiritual revelation word from the Lord God Almighty.

David Day
Executive Director
Teen Challenge Adult Centers of Texas Inc.

A Butterfly Takes Flight

—Lessons from Life—

Norene Gion

Lovett Press International
214-350-1696
ann@lovettconsulting.com

Scripture taken from the New King James Version®.
Copyright © 1982 by Thomas Nelson. Used by permission.
All rights reserved.

Scripture quotations taken from the (NASB®) New American
Standard Bible®, Copyright 1960, 1971, 1977, 1995, 2020 by
the Lockman Foundation. Used by permission. All rights
reserved. www.lockman.org.

Scripture quotations marked (NLT) are taken from the Holy
Bible, copyright © 1996, 2004, 2015 by Tyndale House
Foundation. Used by permission of Tyndale House Publishers,
Carol Stream, Illinois, 60188. All rights reserved.

Scriptures taken from the Holy Bible, New International
Version®, NIV®. Copyright © 1973, 1978, 1984, 2011, by
Biblica Inc.™ Used by permission of Zondervan. All rights
reserved.

Cover artwork created by Mark Marcuson. Used by
permission.
www.Markmarcuson.com
Drawings created by Donna Compton. Used by permission.
www.donnacomptonart.com; donna.compton@me.com

Dedication

I dedicate this book to my children, Brenda Gion Schepler and Curtis Gion; my grandchildren, Luke, Benjamin, Elizabeth, and Hannah Schepler, and Andrew, Samuel, and Anna Gion, and my wonderful in-laws, Jeff Schepler and Janice Gion. You have been supportive of me as I worked on my writing off and on for much of your lives. Thank you.

Acknowledgments

I am so grateful to my friends and prayer partners who have walked with me through this journey, as God opened doors to ministry through Living Waters, Teen Challenge and various church healing groups. Penny and John Kunkel, Laurie and Scott Kerr, Shawn and Raun Lohry, and Karen Bowling are just a few who walked with me.

I especially want to acknowledge Dave and Rogene Argue, both now with the Lord in Heaven, for pastoring and supporting me when I first began ministering at Christ Place Church, Lincoln Nebraska.

Thank you, Donna Compton for the drawings you created for this book. They provide a compelling visual for the content.

Thank you to Ann Lovett Baird of Lovett Press International who guided me through the publishing process. She was a gift from God.

Thank you, Mark Marcuson for allowing me to use your beautiful painting of a butterfly on the front cover.

Foreword

Just as every beautiful butterfly starts its new life concealed and isolated, suspended in darkness as a soft, spineless caterpillar, each one of us must find our strength and God-given backbone. We do this by walking with God and yes, sometimes crawling. The caterpillar has a meltdown inside his cocoon. Every organ and cell of his body turns into a soup of mush called Imaginal cells. But as he is suspended all alone, between heaven and earth, his God-given DNA comes together and realigns as a higher more amazing being.

When it is finally time for him to emerge to display his new identity in the dawn's early light, he has to struggle with all of his might. He knows it is a life-or-death situation. He has been stuck, concealed, dying to old self. But it is now time to allow the resurrection power that has always been within to break forth. He pushes himself forward, one step at a time, he crawls to the top of the opening, spreads his wings to let his brilliant, rainbow colors shine. He rejoices releasing an eternal beacon of light to celebrate overcoming life's most difficult challenge, the transformational process of rebirth.

In Norene Gion's book, *A Butterfly Takes Flight* you will discover the true answers to questions like "Why me?" that you have been asking about life. Norene pulls from the vast, costly treasure chest of wisdom's wealth that she collected through passing her own tests, trials and lessons from life.

No one should have to live in the fear of being hurt physically or emotionally, abandoned or abused by people in their circle of life, who they should be able to trust. Norene graciously opens her heart to you the reader to share the knowledge that she gleaned by overcoming the depths of her pain, disappointments and sorrow.

You will learn how to take wing to arise from the captive pit of despair to be transformed into a Believer in Christ. Norene shares how the things we do in the natural have spiritual parallels. Bad thoughts, attitudes, decisions and habits form negative harmful outlooks on life that can hold you prisoner.

We fearfully wait to be told what to do, never taking the risk to spread our own wings to fly. While in contrast, believing what a loving, life-giving God says about us brings an eternal spring of hope that creates a new Christ-like identity. When we learn to stroll through the garden of life hand-in-hand with the One who created us in His image and likeness, we learn that prayer is not an obligation, discipline or duty, but it is one of life's powerful transformative honors.

Lift your wings, wait for the wind of the Spirit, now spread them wide, let God's spirit catch you up to soar on the breeze as a free, extraordinarily beautiful butterfly.

Dr. Barbie L. Breathitt
Breath of the Spirit Ministries, Inc.
DreamsDecoder.com
DecodeMyDream.com
ASK BARBIE Prophetic Life Coach 972-253-6653

Table of Contents

Introduction

In my early thirties, after getting divorced from an abusive husband, I started a journey of digging deeper into my faith. Though I prayed the prayer of salvation at four-years-old, I had no idea what I was saying. I was terrified. When I was twelve, it was conviction from the Holy Spirit that prompted me to ask Jesus into my heart. Even though I had accepted Christ as my savior, I didn't feel intimate and close to Him.

Several months after my divorce, I was assessing my life and asked myself, "What do you believe? What is true? Is there a God?"

When I truly gave my heart to Him at the age of twelve, I believed He was real because I felt peace and joy at that time. Remembering that, I concluded that God must be real.

I asked myself, "Is the Bible true?"

This was a little harder to believe since I had no concrete proof in my own life I could recall, so I had to accept the Bible by faith.

I remember thinking, "Since there is a God, I must accept that the Bible is His Word, therefore it must be true."

I was raised in church and heard passages from the Bible all my life. I knew what my parents believed; I knew what my church taught, but I didn't know what was true. I didn't know what I believed.

If I accepted that God is real and the Bible is true, I needed to find out what it said. I lived my entire life with first my parents telling me what to do, then my husband telling me what to do. But I needed to read the Bible for myself so I could do whatever it told me to do. However, no one else could dictate to me how to live my life any longer unless they could show me where it was found in scripture. The Bible became my guide for life and this decision totally changed me.

When I began my quest to discover who God is and His instructions for me, I heard from God on a regular basis, first in the Bible, then later from words that came directly to my heart. I began a life of prayer. The Bible says to pray without ceasing and I took that literally. I prayed about everything and God gave me answers.

As I read the Bible, I found promises I felt I could claim as my own. The Bible is the Word of God and He cannot lie so He had to do what He said He would, if I did my part. When I found these scriptures of promise, I called them my own and put the date I claimed them in the margin of my Bible. I fully expected God to do what He said He would, and He did.

Natural Laws Have a Spiritual Parallel

I learned every natural law has a spiritual parallel. I didn't know it at the time but there was a great rift between my head and my heart. All the knowledge I had of God in my head did not affect my life, because it didn't penetrate my heart – that feeling part of me. Symbols are the language of the heart.

I got in the habit of taking long walks and talking to God. He would draw my attention to things in the natural, then tell me what this represented in the spiritual. I also learned I would forget what He said if I didn't write it down, so began to keep a prayer journal, writing down my prayers as well as God's answers.

On one of these walks, I had an experience with a Swallowtail butterfly that changed my life. After that, I experienced the deepest personal walk with God ever. It began a new chapter in my life.

My Hope for You

This book includes life lessons I received from the Lord through the years and recorded in my prayer journals. I hope these will encourage you in your own walk with God. You can trust Him and trust His Word. Claim His promises because they are true.

At the end of each chapter, I have included a place for you to write down your reflections on what the Lord speaks to you from the story and the lesson I learned. I hope this will help you apply my experiences with the Lord to your own journey.

May God bless you as you read, hear what He is saying to you and apply it to your walk with Him.

The Tiger Swallowtail Butterfly

And do not be conformed to this world, but be transformed by the renewing of your mind, that you may prove what is that good and acceptable and perfect will of God.

Romans 12:2, NKJV

Life Lesson

God transformed me into a new creature when I submitted to His view of me. Through an experience with a beautiful butterfly, He taught me how much He loves me and how He views me. He wants me to *believe* I am beautiful in His sight.

****

While hiking in the woods in Nebraska, I saw a very large yellow butterfly just ahead of me. I had never seen one like it before. It was so beautiful, as though each wing had been painted by the artist Himself. I began asking

God to tell it to sit down so I could take a picture of it. The butterfly just kept fluttering and flitting then landing, but just as I would get close enough to get a picture, away it would fly. I followed it through the woods as it stayed on the path that led me to the edge of a pond.

I stood there watching this beautiful butterfly disappear and asked God, "Please, oh please, tell it to come back."

It got so small I wasn't sure I was seeing it at all. *Was it coming back?* I wondered. Yes, it really was getting larger and larger!

I asked God, "Please, oh please let me get a picture."

When the butterfly was on the path it was flitting and fluttering, but now it was flying straight toward me. It flew around me about three times and landed on the rocks beside me. I was holding my breath, not wanting to scare it before I got a picture. I took several with my little camera, and it didn't move – it just sat there.

I had a strong desire to feel the velvet of its wings, so asked the Lord if I could touch this beautiful creature. In awe and wonder I sat down beside it on the rocks. It didn't move. I reached out with the tip of my finger and lightly stroked its body as it opened and closed its wings. I just marveled at its beauty and the fact that God had answered my prayer. Wow! What a moment! Remembering people were waiting on me, I reluctantly left the butterfly. It did not fly off but just sat there as I walked away.

About three months later, I signed up to receive prayer from a team at my church. The team leader said he thought I had something I was supposed to share with them. I remembered the butterfly and told them the above story.

The prayer leader asked me, "How did you feel about the butterfly?"

I said, "I thought it was the most beautiful thing I had ever seen."

He said, "That is how God feels about you."

The fact that God thought I was beautiful was foreign to me. I knew God loved me because the Bible said so. It was hard for me to accept. I realized later that I felt more like a fat caterpillar than a beautiful butterfly.

Then he asked me, "Would you hurt the butterfly?"

"No, I just wanted to touch it."

He said, "That is how God feels about you."

I was speechless! God wanted to touch me?

The leader asked, "How do you think the butterfly felt about you?"

I answered, "Probably pretty scared."

He said, "That is how you feel about God."
I was overcome with emotion. I told the group that I was so surprised as I realized I was afraid of God. I did not know I was really afraid of God. I felt He was someone in Heaven

with a club ready to take me out whenever I messed up, not someone who considered me beautiful and loved me.

As I finished my story, the prayer leader said that God saw me as I saw that butterfly and felt exactly about me the same way I felt about it. I was numb with shock trying to digest the fact that Creator God truly did love me like the Bible said. The leader instructed me to put the butterfly picture in my wallet and to look at it often, as it represented me. I look at it to this day. The butterfly became my symbol of how God viewed me. I seemed to see them everywhere, I went.

Prayer

Oh Lord, continue to teach me. Train me to be the woman You created me to be. Change me into who You say that I am, and not the ugly picture I carry around in my head.

Reflections

What stands out to you in the story?

_____

_____

_____

What is God speaking to your heart through this life
lesson?

_____

_____

_____

My Journal

_____

_____

_____

_____

_____

_____

_____

More Butterflies

He heals the brokenhearted and binds up their wounds.

Psalm 147:3, NKJV

Life Lesson

God used several other interactions with butterflies to reveal my wounded heart. I was surprised I had heart wounds, because I thought I pretty much had things together. I realized how deeply the Lord loves me and how much He wants to heal all my wounds.

****

After receiving prayer and instruction from the church prayer team, I left the next morning to drive to Michigan from Nebraska. I clipped the butterfly picture to my dashboard, so it was easy to see as I traveled down the road. As I drove east along Interstate 80, I had my boombox blasting as I sang along with the praise music.

The Lord spoke to me and said, "Don't be a phony!"

I answered, "I'm not a phony."

He said, "You don't mean what you are singing."

My guilty conscience had to agree with the Lord even as I denied the charge. I repented and vowed to the Lord that I would never again say or sing praises that I didn't mean. I turned off the music.

I decided to exit the Interstate and travel on the backroads so I could see the landscape. It was the beginning of fall weather and I was so excited to see there were hundreds of monarch butterflies flying along the highway. They would fly straight toward the car, catch the updraft, then go over the top. It took my breath as I expected them to crash into the windshield, but they never did. As I thought about the butterflies flying right into the face of danger, trusting the wind dynamics to give them the lift they needed to rise above the oncoming sure death, I knew that was how God wanted me to learn to trust Him. I just needed to obey His direction.

I realized that I am not to let the circumstances of this present life dictate my actions, even when it looks like something fatal is surely going to happen. Like butterflies risking crashing into the windshield that were lifted over the car.

I stopped at a roadside park to eat the sack lunch I packed. No one else was in the park but me. I truly worshipped as I ate my lunch, listened to my boombox and continued to talk out loud to God.

While sitting on my blanket, I suddenly felt prickly all over and saw ants crawling on the blanket. I jumped up to leave. As I was loading the car, I saw a monarch butterfly flitting around. I grabbed my camera wondering if this was another encounter. No, it flew straight into the woods even though I was asking God to tell it to sit down. Suddenly, a carload of teenage boys drove into the park making me feel uneasy, so I jumped in the car, locked the doors, and continued my journey.

The Lord spoke to me as I drove. He asked, "Why are you running from My presence?"

I answered, "I wasn't. The ants were biting me, and the boys made me nervous."

He asked me again, "Why are you running from My presence?"

I finally acknowledged that I got frightened. It was Him I was afraid of, not the ants or the boys.

He then asked, "How did you feel when the butterfly flew away?"

I answered, "Really sad."

He said, "That is how I felt, when you ran from Me."

I was so surprised He would want to spend time with me. I recalled the prayer session after my first butterfly encounter and remembered that fear of God was one of the issues I was dealing with.

I asked God, "Will I ever be free of unreasonable fear? Please forgive me for running from You. I will find another park, stop and stay in Your presence as long as You want me to."

I did find another roadside park, and again took my blanket, camera and went to meet alone with God. It was hot by this time and where I was sitting there wasn't a breath of air stirring. The mosquitoes were buzzing as I sat with my arms crossed waiting for God to say something. I waited and waited. I heard nothing and saw nothing.

It was getting on in the day and I had a hotel room reserved, so I had to get on the road. I quickly forgot the butterflies and my conversation with God.

The next day in Michigan I stopped at another roadside park. As I was getting back in my car, I noticed a monarch butterfly sitting between two flowers right in front of my car. I carefully put my hand under it and found it was dead! I left it, but before I could leave, I remembered butterflies mean something. I picked it up again carefully and put it in the car. As I drove away with the dead butterfly, I began to cry.

The Lord asked, "Did the butterfly give you any pleasure?"

I answered, "Of course not; it was dead!"

He said, "Neither did you give Me pleasure when you came back into My presence yesterday. I gave you a personality I enjoy, and I like to interact with you; but you were like the dead butterfly."

I said, "I was waiting on You to speak."

God answered, "So was I. "

I never knew God enjoyed me talking to Him; not simply praying for things but communicating what was going on in my life; how I felt about things and what I thought. At that moment, my heart was being filled with His love.

I drove on to my brother's house and spent the night. The next day we drove to the upper peninsula of Michigan to go camping. When we arrived at the campground, a storm was brewing. I saw a butterfly fluttering in the rocks by the road that was hurt and could not fly. I lifted it and set it in the grass, as I prayed for it. I didn't know what else to do for a hurt butterfly, and the storm was upon us. I ran back to the camper before the rain started.

At the end of my visit while driving home, I asked God to tell me the message of the hurt butterfly.

He said, "You too have been wounded but I am going to heal you."

Again, I was shocked because I was not aware of how wounded my heart was. In fact, before I encountered the butterflies, I thought I had it pretty well all together. Little did I know I was going into the spiritual chrysalis stage of life, quietly set apart and developing into something altogether different than what I was before.

God gave me visuals to penetrate my heart because the knowledge in my head was not reaching the wounds in my heart. You see the language of the heart is symbolism, so God was using symbols to teach me His truth and to heal my broken image of myself. I began to accept myself just the way God made me. I still look at that picture of the butterfly from time to time and remember how I came to know God's love for me through His beautiful creature.

Prayer

Oh Lord don't let me forget this life lesson of your unending love and care for me. The way you called me aside to be alone with You for times of intimacy, the way you healed my broken wounded heart. Thank You.

Reflections

What stands out to you in the story?

_____

_____

_____

What is God speaking to your heart through this life
lesson?

_____

_____

_____

My Journal

_____

_____

_____

_____

_____

_____

_____

The Approaching Storm

You know how to interpret the appearance of the sky, but
you cannot interpret the signs of the times?

Matthew 16:2b, NIV

Life Lesson

The Lord taught me that if I am prepared by listening to Him, I can enjoy the adventures of life without fear. Even if I don't know the result of the storm I am walking through, I can trust the Lord, by faith that He will protect me.

****

The darkening sky and the sound of distant thunder alerted me to the approaching storm. The latest weather report showed the radar tracking this line of thunderstorms for several hours. The center of the storm was headed over Lake Michigan but would not come ashore in Indiana.

On impulse, I grabbed my umbrella and jacket, and with a sense of adventure, headed for the beach. I felt like a kid going to a parade; wanting to be sure I got there before it started. The storm was moving fast, and I didn't want to miss it. It was a hot sunny day, so the beach was packed. Going toward the beach was like trying to swim upstream against the flow of people who were leaving. Parents were pressing their children to hurry before the storm arrived. I tried to tell them this was only the edge of the storm and it was not coming ashore, but my voice was snatched away by the wind, so no one was listening to me. I walked toward the beach.

Under the darkening sky, the water looked grey green with white caps crashing against the shore. It looked more like an ocean than a land-locked lake. The beach was deserted now except for three teenage boys who are playing in the water. They defied the elements and the power of the waves as they jumped into each approaching white cap with great delight and abandon. I could hear their yells of excitement over the sound of the wind and water as they enjoyed the challenge. I, too, felt excitement, as I watched the awesome power of this fast-moving storm in its race across the giant screen sky. The radar proved correct. The storm was about thirty miles north and moving to the east; it didn't come ashore where I was.

What did the teens and I have in common? We were not afraid of the storm. In fact, all of us enjoyed it. As teenagers, they felt invincible, and I had knowledge others did not have because I knew the projected path of the storm. With my own eyes, I saw the storm headed toward the lake as it was tracked by the radar. Also, the experts with years of training, knowledge and experience, predicted the path of the storm and I accepted their word by faith. I have faced and weathered many storms in the past and have learned to trust the accuracy of radar. My knowledge was not based on the visible elements of rolling dark clouds backlit by lightning, or the dropping temperature and strong gusts of wind. Based on the radar, I was prepared for the weather with a jacket and umbrella ready, in case it did shower.

The people at the beach were afraid of the storm. They had not consulted the radar. They were unprepared and just had clothes for the beach. The only thing they had to go by was their senses, what the sky looked like, and the feel of the dropping temperature and gusting wind.

How do we discern the signs of the times? Is it not by the same method I used to discern the approaching storm? We consult the ever-true radar of scripture, seek direction from the Holy Spirit and check our conclusions with people we trust who have training and experience in interpreting the scripture and the signs of the times. We walk by faith and not by sight. It was faith in what I heard that gave me peace to sit and watch the storm as others scurried away.

Always listen for the voice of the Lord. You never know what God is going to use to teach you.

Prayer

Oh Lord, just as I knew the storm would not come my way because I knew where it was going, help me interpret the signs of the times so I am not afraid of dark clouds of an approaching storm. Let me never forget that You are my shield and defender. You have a plan for me, to give me a future and a hope. Let me stand in the face of the storms of life with great peace. Let me leap into the whitecaps with abandon as the teenagers did, taking delight in the challenge.

Reflections

What stands out to you in the story?

_____

_____

_____

What is God speaking to your heart through this life lesson?

_____

_____

_____

My Journal

_____

_____

_____

_____

_____

_____

The Jack Pine Tree

Everything that can endure fire, you shall put through the fire, and it shall be clean; and it shall be purified with the water of purification . . .

Numbers 31:23, NKJV

Life Lesson

Through the years, God has shown me that He is a consuming fire that can equip us for all that He wants for us in this life. The trials of fire may not be very fun while we are going through them, but once we have traveled through the fire, we can burst into new life.

****

While camping with my brother and his wife in the upper peninsula of Michigan, we took a hike along the trails in a nearby park. There were signs explaining the different vegetation along the path, but the one that caught my interest was the Jack Pine. The Jack Pinecones are small with tightly closed petals covered by a thick waxy substance. God created this tree to re-forest after a fire. The sign gave a full explanation of what happens to the land after the vegetation has been destroyed. The seeds within the cone are released as the cone is burned, so this tree can only reproduce after a fire. The waxy substance on the outside of the cone protects it from insects eating it, or water getting in and making it decay. It also acts as a starter for the fire. As the cones are destroyed the seeds are released.

We wanted to see what happens when the cones are burned, so we took several back to camp with us. As the day faded while we were sitting around the campfire, I carefully put one of the pinecones on top of the fire so I could watch it open. It wasn't long before the wood under the cone burned so the cone fell into the bottom of the fire, and we forgot all about it. As the evening wore on, the fire burned out until we could not see even a tiny spark left. Like I said, we had totally forgotten the Jack Pinecone as we were getting ready for bed. Suddenly the cone literally exploded. Red hot glowing seeds scattered many feet in every direction and popped like firecrackers. It was like a beautiful July 4th celebration in the total dark of night – a fire light shower going in every direction.

As I thought on what I had witnessed I realized Christians are, at times, like the Jack Pinecone. We become crusted with things that need to be burned off, to release His spirit dwelling within us. He must throw us into the fire to burn away all that is not of Him. The seeds were not released until the fire had cooled and no sparks were left. If the seeds had been released earlier, they would have been destroyed along with the pinecone. The seeds flew many feet in every direction to accomplish their task of re-forestation.

We don't always understand why we must go through hard or painful things, but like the Jack Pinecone, after we have survived the fire, we are free to be used. So, when you feel the heat, don't resist; remember God has you in the fire to burn off all that is not of Him so He can release all He has hidden inside you. Here are some scriptures that speak of the consuming fire of God.

*The sight of the glory of the Lord was like a consuming fire
on the top of the mountain in the eyes of the children of
Israel.*

Exodus 24:17, NKJV

For the Lord your God is a consuming fire, a jealous God.

Deuteronomy 4:24, NKJV

Prayer

*Oh Lord give me the courage to yield to your all-
consuming fire.*

Reflections

What stands out to you in the story?

_____

_____

_____

_____

What is God speaking to your heart through this life lesson?

_____

_____

_____

_____

My Journal

_____

_____

_____

_____

_____

A Butterfly Takes Flight

Prisms and Light

Let your light shine before men in such a way that they may see your good works and glorify your Father who is in heaven.

Matthew 5:16, NASB

Life Lesson

All of us have unique giftings that are bestowed on us by the Lord. When we let His light shine through us and we use the gifts He has given us to fulfill our purpose, we can shine His light in a dark world in a powerful way.

****

While praying for a young man in my fellowship group, I saw a prism with the light shining through showing the array of colors. I prayed what I was seeing. I was challenged by another person in the group about the allegory of us being prisms as opposed to mirrors.

I knew what I saw was a prism, so after the meeting I researched the properties of prisms and the reference to light in the Bible. I was taking a writing class at the university at the time where the professor gave us an assignment to write an allegory. Since I was already investigating prisms and light, I chose this for my topic. Below is the allegory that I wrote.

****

Light is the very source of life. Green plants, using photosynthesis, combine carbon dioxide, water and light energy to manufacture glucose and oxygen. This glucose is stored inside the plant and provides food for itself or other animals. Some animals don't eat plants but other animals; however, these other animals eat plants, so without the energy from light, eventually life would cease.

Sir Isaac Newton learned to separate visible light into a spectrum of colors by passing it through a prism. Then he took another prism and passed the separated light back through, creating white light again. This proved light is made of several different colors ranging from violet at one end of the spectrum to red at the other.

The most powerful rays of light are not visible. The violet end of the spectrum where the gamma rays are is not visible to our eyes and is where x-ray light waves are located. On the other end, or the red end, are the microwaves and radio waves. Photosynthesis absorbs both the violet and red rays of light and reflects the rest, or the green tinted rays, thus the green color of plants.

Long before any of this was understood by man, Jesus was referred to as the light of the world. In John's gospel, Jesus is quoted

> . . . *I am the light of the world; he who follows Me shall not walk in the darkness but shall have the light of life.*

John 8:12, NASB

As in the physical, there is no hope for life without light, the same is true in the spiritual, there is no hope for a spiritual life without Jesus.

In the recording of Jesus' Sermon on the Mount, in Matthew 5, He refers to his followers as light as well.

> *You are the light of the world* . . .

Matthew 5:14, NASB

and again, the instruction to:

Let your light shine before men in such a way that they may see your good works and glorify your Father who is in heaven.

Matthew 5:16, NASB

Now Jesus has already called himself the light and the light of life, so he is not talking about a different light. He is referring to himself or His spirit. I believe in these scriptures He is calling His followers, later to be called His church, to be prisms so the beauty of His light could shine through to the spiritual darkness around.

I see the different rays of light producing beautiful colors as it flows through the prism, as being parallel to the various manifestations of the Spirit in the Christian life. Just as the beauty of light is not appreciated until you see the rainbow through the prism, so the beauty of God is not appreciated or understood until it flows through the believer.

The way the Spirit manifests itself in the church is explained in Romans 12:6-8 where the various gifts of the spirit are listed. These include teaching, prophesying, encouraging or exhorting, giving, and showing mercy. Just as there are many colors but one light, I Corinthians says:

There are different kinds of spiritual gifts, but the same
Spirit is the source of them all.

I Corinthians 12:4, NLT

What does the Christian have to do to obtain these gifts in their life? Well, using the prism as the example, for the rainbow to be seen, the prism must stay in the light and not in the shadow. It also must stay clean. If there is any dirt or smudges on the prism it inhibits the light flow. In a Christian's life, the smudges are called sin. In I John we are told,

If we confess our sins, He is faithful and righteous
to forgive us our sins and to cleanse us from all
unrighteousness

I John 1:9, NASB

The prism can do nothing within itself to separate the light, however when it was made, it was constructed in such a way that the light rays are bent when they come through, thus separating them so they can be seen. When Jesus performs His redeeming work within a person's life, He restructures the person spiritually so that His glory can shine through. The prism had to yield itself to the glass cutter to be reshaped so we too must yield to God to be fashioned, to be usable, and to allow His gifting to manifest itself in our lives. The prism also must stay in the light. James advises,

Draw near to God and He will draw near to you.

James 4:8, NASB

Therefore, it is through no special effort or power of the Christian, but the power of Almighty God that produces the tireless love and compassion of the Sister Theresas in this world. They are simply prisms or channels of God's love, beauty, and power changing the world around them.

God, in his wisdom and desire to reveal Himself to man chose His church to show the world the power of His love and beauty. Isaac Newton thought he had discovered something totally new, but God knew all along. He allowed Isaac to create a physical example of a spiritual truth.

****

The professor told me he was profoundly moved by this allegory. He told me that other Christians tried to write their allegory to prove the Bible, but it had never worked before. He complimented me and said he couldn't find any holes or flaws in the premise of this paper. I was proud to receive an A on this assignment.

Prayer

Thanks, Lord, for letting me be a prism, and teaching me through the very nature You created. May I always be open to learn from You.

Reflections

What stands out to you in the story?

_____

_____

_____

_____

What is God speaking to your heart through this life
lesson?

_____

_____

_____

_____

My Journal

_____

_____

_____

_____

_____

Light and Shadows

No one lights a lamp and then puts it under a basket.
Instead, a lamp is placed on a stand, where it gives light to
everyone in the house. In the same way, let your good
deeds shine out for all to see, so that everyone will praise
your heavenly Father.

Matthew 5:15-16. NLT

Life Lessons

Through my life I have prayed for missionaries who go around the world disseminating God's light. I am privileged to support those who risk their lives in order to spread the Gospel. He has also shown me that all of us are missionaries to our communities, business associates and anyone we come in contact with. God wants us to be a light to the world.

****

Early one Sunday morning as I was on my way to church in Chicago, I noticed a misty haze that engulfed the landscape, which the increasing light and warmth of the sun was burning off. I remembered traveling in an airplane and flying through a cloud layer to break into the sun. The thought occurred to me that the sun was not any brighter, or warmer than it ever is. The misty haze was merely filtering the sun's rays.

I visualized mountains, plains, seashores and deserts and the difference in the sun's intensity in each place. Yet the sun does not change. Its heat and light are always the same. I see the world as a globe from a great distance and yet, as if through a telescope. I get close-up pictures of the individual parts. The sun is always shining brightly, ever the same. In some places the sun is muted and obscured by smog, which is smoke and other manmade pollution. In other places heavy fog filters the light. Yet the smog, heavy fog and an occasional storm cloud cannot keep out the light or cut off the warmth. Places closer to the sun make it appear brighter and hotter; however, the sun never shines any differently. It is simply the close proximity to the earth that makes the sun feel warmer and appear brighter.

I visualized a cloud over a section of the world that was so thick and black, the light could not penetrate it. The cloud was so thick that not even the sun, moon or stars could penetrate the blackness. As I watched I saw a small beam of light moving into the darkness. The sun was ever the same above the hovering cloud. As the light moved across the black land, it faded and glowed brighter by turns. As it moved from place-to-place tiny pin pricks of light appeared in the darkness. Each little light had a golden thread penetrating the dark cloud connecting it to the sun. The threads of light looked almost solid.

The light and dark in nature is similar to people's knowledge of the truth and God's light versus the darkness. In some places people have access to the full truth, light, love and power of Jesus Christ, like the sun shining in the desert. In other places the light and truth are not obscured, but because of position, they don't receive the full benefit of the sun. They are off to the right or left of center. In other places the pollution and stench of the sins of the people rise from the earth and obscure the sun. The light and warmth still penetrate but the edges of the sun are blurred, hazy and the sun's definition is not clear. The truth becomes blurred, obscure, and is hard to discern or define.

The black cloud is not earthly, caused by the weather, but an evil so thick that it absorbs all the light. However, as the heat rays from the sun cannot be totally blocked, so the heat of God's love penetrates the spiritual cloud. I realize the light being carried into the darkness is a large handheld lantern representing God's truth message, which must be carried into the darkness.

The hand-held lantern is constructed so the strongest wind and rain cannot put it out.

I ask the Lord what the dimming and brightening of the light represent.

He explains, "The brightness of the lantern is directly affected by the prayers of the people. When prayers of intercession are offered, the light burns brightly, but when the prayers cease, the light grows dim."

As I watch the little lights continue to appear. More and more golden threads of truth connect to the sun through the cloud. I ask the Lord if it is the messenger carrying the truth lantern, or the intercessors causing the pin pricks of light to appear. His answer is clear.

He says, "It takes both."

If we sit and pray for the unbelieving people in darkness but never send a messenger, they will never hear the truth of the Gospel. Likewise, if we send only food, clothing and humanitarian aid, but never the light of truth, the darkness will not be penetrated. Also, if we send the messenger with the truth and fail to support them in prayer, the message of truth will eventually grow so dim it will have little effect. The messenger being sent with the lantern, and the prayers of intercession for the messenger and the people bring a harvest of golden lights.

As I watch, the little lights join the lantern light as they move together into the darkness, in a rhythmic like dance. They weave in and out, back and forth lighting more and more lamps, making a golden canopy of light, as each thread penetrates the black cloud and connects with the son.

Prayer

Father thank you for the opportunity to spread light to the world. Through my prayers and support for missionaries and ministers, people learn of Your love and grace. Show me how I can spread Your light and grace in every situation in my life.

Reflections

What stands out to you in the story?

_____

_____

_____

_____

What is God speaking to your heart through this life lesson?

_____

_____

_____

_____

My Journal

_____

_____

_____

_____

Ladybugs

I can do all things through Christ who strengthens me.

Philippians 4:13, NKJV

Life Lessons

Through my life God has taught me that no matter what I face, He will always strengthen me. He will not be offended when I tell Him how I feel about my circumstances or a situation. He is always there to walk me through whatever trial I have.

****

As a single mom of two kids, I had to be responsible for everything from discipline, financial expenses, maintenance for the house, the car, and anything else we needed. As I read the Bible daily, it became the blueprint for my life. If the Bible said do it, I did it to the best of my ability.

I found Isaiah 54 that says God is the husband of the widow. My church pastor was teaching on the roles of the family. He said the father, or husband was responsible for providing for the family financially, doing the yard and mechanical work about the house, and the biggie, disciplining the children. The wife or mother was to keep the house clean, do the cooking, take care of the kids while the husband was at work, the typical family. This was confusing to me since there was only me to do everything. Based on the pastor's teaching, when I found this scripture, I thought I understood what I could depend on God for. He would have all the father's responsibility for my kids, as well as being responsible for me as my husband.

For your creator will be your husband, the Lord of Heaven's Armies is His name! He is your redeemer, the Holy One of Israel, the God of all the earth.

Isaiah 54:5, NLT

It was springtime and our yard had fleas that infested the dog then got into the house. This was the confusing part for me. I was responsible for all the husband's yard work, as well as the laundry and house cleaning from the wife's list. One Saturday in the spring I mowed and sprayed the entire yard with bug killer. The wind was blowing so the spray got all over me and I reeked of insecticide. As I put everything away in the tool shed, I was looking forward to washing my hair and taking a bubble bath, so I headed to the house. When I got to the patio, I noticed my rose bush was covered with aphids. I turned around to go back to the tool shed to get the rose dust. Suddenly, I stopped in the middle of the yard and realized how tired I was as I stood there.

I looked up toward heaven and said, "God what kind of husband are you anyway? No man wants his wife to smell of insecticide. If you were any kind of husband, you would be bringing me flowers. You know how much I love roses. Besides this isn't my job anyway."

So, I turned back, went into the house, ignoring the aphids and took my bubble bath.

The next evening my son who was in junior high at the time, called me from the back yard, "Mom come look at these lady bugs!"

I walked out to find the rose bush covered in ladybugs feasting on the aphids. This rose bush bloomed only in early spring and did not bloom again until the next year. However, for the rest of that year, the blooms just stayed on the bush. The flowers did not wilt unless I cut them. The next spring it returned to an early spring rose, but for that summer I had roses every day if I wanted them.

I do not recommend talking to God in the frustrated way that I did, however He does tell us to test him and see if He won't prove himself, which is what he was doing for me. He wanted me to know He loved me and would take care of me. He would even give me things for my pleasure like the roses.

The lesson I learned from the ladybug was God knows what is in our hearts and when we express it to Him, He is not offended. In fact, He can't deal with our hearts until we know what is there. Also, the promises in the Bible are there for me; both old and new testament, so I can claim them, and He honors that. He has my back.

Prayer

Thank you, Lord, for being my everything.

Reflections

What stands out to you in the story?

_____

_____

_____

_____

What is God speaking to your heart through this life lesson?

_____

_____

_____

_____

My Journal

_____

_____

_____

_____

_____

The Butterfly House

"For I know the plans I have for you," says the Lord. "They are plans for good and not for disaster, to give you a future and a hope."

Jeremiah 29:11, NKJV

Life Lesson

God has shown me that He is the perfect provider for everything I need. I don't need to strive to find greener pastures. Because I am strong-willed, sometimes I work too hard to make things happen. Ultimately, in some cases, it's like I'm beating my head against the wall. When I back up and behold God for all He is and how He feels about me, I realize He has given me everything I need and more.

****

While on a mission trip to England I stayed an extra week to do some sightseeing. The hosts where I was staying heard about my butterfly petting experience and told me about a butterfly house outside of London in Syon Park. I took the subway and transferred a couple times to get there, but it was worth it. The Syon Estate was built in the 1500s and is one of the few great houses left. From the residence you could see an open meadow looking toward the Thames River where boats were visible. The meadow was full of little yellow wildflowers. Since it is private land and visitors are not allowed to take pictures of the property, I had to capture it with words.

The sky was clear and blue with a few white clouds. Trees were growing along the Thames on the other side of the meadow but at the bend in the river there was a break in the trees. There was probably a dock there since the members of the Syon House, which has belonged to the Duke of Northumberland in the Percy family for hundreds of years, traveled back and forth to London by river.

The Butterfly House had a perfect environment for butterflies. The buildings were comprised of three metal frames with heavy plastic walls, roof and door. The entry way contained a heavy plastic door into the butterfly area, so the butterflies could not escape. In this perfect environment, flowers of all kinds provided the butterflies different varieties of nectar, lots of green foliage with shadows for the night moths. A running stream with a bubbling fountain flowed through the house. Dishes of sugar water with plastic scratchers for butterflies to land on and drink were scattered throughout the building. The butterflies of all descriptions and colors were almost tame.

While walking and enjoying the many different varieties of butterflies, I noticed another tourist, a rather large man, who had a butterfly alight on his back.

He began yelling, "Get it off! Get it off!"

The people with him did not want to touch it either. I put my open hand in front of the butterfly and it lightly stepped into my palm. I held it for the longest time and people kept asking if I wanted them to take my picture with my camera, so I got several good shots. The butterfly seemed content to let me carry it as I walked around, enjoying God's beauty. Like the first butterfly that I held, this one did not fly away from me. I finally put my hand beside a flower and the butterfly stepped off.

I noticed some of the butterflies trying to get out of the Butterfly House. They were flying into the see-through wall, repeatedly. They didn't quit but kept hitting the plastic over and over. I wanted to stop them but felt helpless. If they escaped, they wouldn't survive. But how do you communicate with a butterfly?

I asked the Lord, why they were doing that.

He said, "That is how you are at times. I have provided everything you need for life, but you keep wanting what is just outside the door, or down the street. You feel you know what you need better than I do. I have you in the best place for you at this time in your life, but you keep pushing against the wall, trying to get out so you can get on with your life. The life, the one you have planned, is not what I purposed for you."

I made a choice to see all the wonderful things God had for me like the butterflies in the Butterfly House. I sat and quieted my soul to enjoy God's provision just for me. As I enjoyed the environment, I recognized many of the butterflies' provisions that God had provided for me.

Prayer

Forgive me for my ungrateful heart, strong-willed ways and striving for something different than what You have planned for me. Thank you, Lord, for your love and provision.

Reflections

What stands out to you in the story?

_____

_____

_____

_____

What is God speaking to your heart through this life lesson?

_____

_____

_____

_____

My Journal

_____

_____

_____

_____

Absent Daddy

He heals the brokenhearted and binds up their wounds.

Psalm 147:3, NKJV

Life Lesson

Sometimes traumatic events that we need Jesus to heal, are hidden in our psyche. The Lord has taught me how powerful this can be, not only for me, but others who I have prayed for. God wants our hearts to be totally whole and healed, so that wounds don't hold us back from the richest life possible.

****

I attended a conference in Michigan by myself because none of my friends could attend. The conference was held at a university with the attendees staying in the dorms. I had a roommate who I had not met before who was also attending alone.

While getting acquainted in our room the first night, she said, "I think you have a memory God wants to heal."

I was unfamiliar with the memory healing ministry at that time, so didn't know what to expect.

As soon as she spoke, I was taken instantly into a vision of my brother and me, and my emotions as a three-year-old, while still being aware of my adult self. It reminded me of watching a play or movie where I can feel the emotions of the character performing but I'm still aware of being a spectator.

Growing up, my mother was alone with three kids: a six-year-old, three-year-old, and a baby. Our house was not far from the railroad track and from time-to-time men who were *riding the rails* would come to our door asking for food. My mother would immediately make my brother and me come in the house and she would lock the doors. She would then fry bacon and eggs or make biscuits and gravy, whatever she had, and feed them on a tin plate with a cup of coffee in a tin cup.

In my vision, my brother, who I called *Brother*, and I were running around in the fenced front yard of our small house, playing, when the gate opened, and a strange man walked in. The gate slammed shut as my heart began to race, and I screamed "Mother!" as I ran toward the house.

You see, she told us if a man comes in the yard, we should immediately run to the house and get her.

I couldn't believe it, but this man was chasing me. I was terrified. He caught me and was holding me tightly. Kicking and screaming and crying for Mother, she finally came out to rescue me, I thought. But not so; she was angry with me. I wondered what had I done?

She said, "This is your Daddy. Give him a kiss."

"What is a Daddy?" I asked.

In 1943 there were no daddies in our neighborhood, only mommies, grandmas and grandpas. All the daddies were in the army or working at necessary draft exempt jobs. Therefore, I didn't know what a daddy was. I couldn't understand why when I did what Mother had always told us, I got in trouble. In my short life I found it was always best to do what she wanted, so I spent my life attempting to please her.

Still in Daddy's arms, we were in a tight circle with Mother facing Daddy and Daddy holding me. The adult me noticed how good looking and young my dad was. Suddenly, I saw Jesus standing between Mother and Daddy looking right at me.

He said, "Look into your daddy's eyes."

Love just poured out of his beautiful blue eyes. For the first time in my memory, the young me, as well as the adult me, knew my daddy loved me. Trauma from this event had blocked me from receiving any affection from my dad my whole life. However, the love from Daddy's eyes brought healing to my heart as the trauma of the terror left. This was the first of many such memory healing experiences. I've also prayed for others to receive this type of healing.

I had no memory of this event until my roommate said she thought Jesus wanted to heal me. Instantly the memory reel started to play, as I watched and experienced the event both as the child in terror and the adult calmly watching. Jesus came into that event and healed my trauma.

Prayer

Thank you, Jesus for not allowing the buried memory to remain, to give trauma a place in my life.

Reflections

What stands out to you in the story?

_____

_____

_____

_____

What is God speaking to your heart through this life lesson?

_____

_____

_____

_____

My Journal

_____

_____

_____

_____

_____

The Oil Lamp

You are the light of the world. A city on a hill cannot be hidden. Neither do people light a lamp and put it under a bowl. Instead they put it on its stand, and it gives light to everyone in the house. In the same way, let your light shine before men that they may see your good deeds and praise your Father in heaven.

Matthew 5:14-16, NIV

Life Lesson

As Christians, we are a light to an unenlightened world. The Lord showed me how to be a light to the world around me by demonstrating His love, mercy and grace to others. This is not a natural action for human beings, so to demonstrate to the world who God is, we need to be continually filled with the Holy Spirit and keep our fire of faith burning.

****

The construction of an oil lamp is simple. The reservoir holds the oil, a wick conducts the oil to the flame, and a chimney or globe protects the flame, yet allows enough air in so the flame can burn steadily. Oil lamps are made of many different materials, some are opaque and others clear, but all have a place to store the oil.

A Christian is like a spiritual oil lamp. When we give our lives to the Lord, the Holy Spirit comes to reside inside us. Like the oil lamp, we have a reservoir where the Holy Spirit resides. The wick, although small, is a major part of the lamp, and is constructed of many tightly knitted cotton strands. The wick acts as a conduit to bring the oil from the depth of the reservoir to the flame. If the wick has been saturated with something other than oil, it cannot be a conductor, and the lamp will not burn correctly. If the wick is frayed and has loose strands, the flame will flicker and smoke, so the wick must be trimmed periodically. An interesting phenomenon is the wick is not consumed by the burning, only the oil. Likewise, the Christian keeps the flame going through prayer and communion with the Father. We daily get our infilling of the Holy Spirit through our time with Him and our worship. If we are not careful, we will allow distractions to dominate our time and interfere with our communion with God, so our light does not burn as brightly. Daily we must pay attention to what we allow into our lives.

The oil lamp's chimney protects the flame from the elements and allows oxygen to feed the flame so it will burn steadily. The chimney surrounds the flame but is crystal clear so the light can shine forth. Because of its shape, the beauty of the flame is enhanced, and the light appears brighter. The glass is especially made to withstand heat. During use the residue from the burning oil, fingerprints, and smoke builds on the chimney, requiring regular cleaning. As the chimney we need the Lord's protection over our lives so the enemy can't come and blow us out. We need to be sure our sins are confessed so we are clean, with no sin smudges to dull our light.

Lamps come in all shapes and sizes. Some are large and ornate to light an entire room, others are small handheld lamps that give off enough light to see your next step. Each type of lamp is constructed for a special purpose. Some lamps are constructed to withstand the fiercest storms, mounted on poles in the street to light the night. Lots of different lamps have common properties.

Like the different types of lamps, in the Body of Christ we have many different purposes. We are not all called to the same tasks, but all are called to be filled, equipped and go forth letting His light show through us.

Although the construction of an oil lamp is not complex, it requires regular attention. The flame from a wick that needs to be trimmed will flicker and smoke. If the chimney is not cleaned regularly, soot will build inside until the light grows dim. An unattended lamp will eventually use all the oil in the reservoir, and the light will go out.

The Lord uses the oil lamp parable to teach us to make sure we have enough oil of the Holy Spirit stored for the future. We do not know the exact time when we will need to go out and meet our bridegroom, Jesus.

Then the kingdom of heaven will be like ten bridesmaids who took their lamps and went to meet the bridegroom.

Five of them were foolish and five were wise. The five who were foolish didn't take enough oil for their lamps, but the other five were wise enough to take along extra oil.

Matthew25:1-4, NLT

The most important thing about a lamp is the flame. The flame shines forth in the darkness lighting the way, drawing all to its brightness. But the flame cannot continue without the fuel of the oil. Our brightness lighting darkness in the world needs the constant infilling of the Holy Spirit.

Prayer

Come light my lamp, Lord Jesus. Fill me daily with the oil of your Holy Spirit. Let there be no smudge or darkness in me. Cleanse me from deceit, envy, anger, or anything hindering Your light shining brightly for all the world to see.

Reflections

What stands out to you in the story?

_____

_____

_____

_____

What is God speaking to your heart through this life lesson?

_____

_____

_____

_____

My Journal

_____

_____

_____

_____

Early Morning Dew

In the mouth of a fool is a rod of pride, But the lips of the wise will preserve them.

Proverbs 14:3, NKJV

Life Lesson

Sometimes in my life, my pride gets in the way of being covered with God and refreshed by Him. He has taught me many lessons about not being too headstrong, leaning on my own understanding or what I think is best. I don't have to always be striving and making things happen. I can let Him renew and refresh me.

****

I raced the sun to the top of the hill and won. I got there before first light. Sitting on the fence to catch my breath, I waited for the sun to catch me. The first streaks of light reflected off something shiny on the ground. I wondered if it was a ring, but on closer inspection, I saw it was not a diamond, but dew drops. Everything was damp, including my shoes from my run through the grass. Dew had fallen equally on everything.

One particularly broad blade of grass had five drops of water shining in the first light. It was almost flat on the ground, bent and cupped on the edges. The drops had not run together but were still in droplets. I looked to see if any of the other grass had such an early morning treasure. Most of the grass was narrow and standing upright.

I got off the fence so I could feel the grass with my hands. All of it was damp, except the crabgrass seed head, which was straight and tall on its high stem, and totally dry.

That made me think about myself when I am headstrong and proud. Then, I am dry like the crabgrass seed head. It's so much better to be covered with God's morning dew.

God uses all creation to get our attention if we will just open our eyes and hearts. He longs to bless and care for us. He enjoys intimate conversations with us, even as we notice water drops of the early morning dew.

As it got lighter, I kept looking back to watch the diamond dew on this one blade of grass, which was bent and cupped as if waiting expectantly. Yes, the dew had fallen on everything the same, but only stayed to refresh that which was open to receive it. My heart was touched as I saw God's grace reflected in the dew, covering everything. God speaks to me through ordinary everyday things when I watch and listen.

So, let us press on, press on to know the Lord. For as surely as the dawn He will come. And as the dew drops kiss the morning grass, so, He will come to His own.

Adapted from Hosea 6:3

Prayer

Oh God, I repent of my proud, straight, head above the crowd, I can handle anything attitude. I bend low before you so I too can receive and retain your renewing Holy Spirit. Come and fill my cupped life – refresh and restore me with your early morning dew.

Reflections

What stands out to you in the story?

_____

_____

_____

_____

What is God speaking to your heart through this life lesson?

_____

_____

_____

_____

My Journal

_____

_____

_____

_____

The Stew Pot

I baptize you with water for repentance. But after me comes one who is more powerful than I, whose sandals I am not worthy to carry. He will baptize you with the Holy Spirit and fire.

Matthew 3:11, NIV

Life Lesson

God wants us to influence our communities with His love, which we can do when we keep the heat of His fire burning in us. His fire that deepens our prayers and keeps us intimate with Him can warm up the world around us too.

****

Walking in the city, I had a heightened sense of the spirit world and realized how much evil there was all around. At the same time, I was also aware I was protected and had nothing to fear. I felt like I was in a bubble that the evil could not penetrate. In fact, I could go anywhere at will and the evil had to give way. I felt such joy to know his protection. I asked the Lord to show me what His protection is like and immediately thought of a steam bubble. Later He showed me more about the steam bubble.

It was August and being a simple farm girl at heart, I was busy canning tomatoes, beans, corn, all the produce of the garden. The next few days as I dropped the tomatoes in the boiling water and watched how quickly the skin popped, I kept pondering the bubble, and asking God to show me more. In my mind's eye I saw a pot of cold stew, you know the thick congealed kind. I saw the cold vegetables trapped in the stew, unable to move. The stew was placed over a low heat and the law of physics came into play. The stew closest to the source of heat on the bottom and sides of the pot converted to liquid. As this first liquid got hotter and hotter, it turned to steam, forced its way around and through the rest of the stew, and escaped in bubbles on the top. In my mind's eye, I continued to watch with great fascination as the stew gradually warmed to liquid and began to gently boil as the steam created bubbles.

I knew the congealed stew was the world, specifically my community. The flame represented the Holy Spirit. I started to pray for the Lord to increase the heat so others could become warm. I realized it might get uncomfortable, but I needed to yield to the heat. As others become warm the law of spiritual physics would take over and everything around them would become warm too. Eventually, the stew would start to simmer as all God's people turned to a liquid and became steam. As I continued to mediate on the simmering stew pot, I realized the heat was perfect. It was not too high, which would cause the stew to burn, nor was it too low, which would allow the stew to remain in its congealed state.

Then I remembered the evil I sensed in the city and knew if our city became a boiling pot filled with the Holy Spirit, something would be done to cool things off. I asked the Lord what we could expect to happen to try and cool off the boiling pot. The answer was exciting. I saw the stew happily simmering and boiling and popping and the vegetables rolling in the liquid all jumbled together. When a fresh batch of cold, raw potatoes, and tomatoes were dumped into the stew, the cool penetrated the liquid, and the boiling momentarily stopped. The sides of the pot remained hot enough to bubble.

Again, I remembered the law of physics. Heat is more powerful and always overcomes cold. Put another way, the cold cannot stay in the presence of heat. It will either get hot or get out of the way. If the potatoes and tomatoes were dumped in the middle of a boiling pot, and the source of heat remained constant, the heat would eventually release the liquid stored in the vegetables and they too would become softened and warm. Since a potato is ninety percent water, and a tomato has an even greater liquid content, it takes less than one minute for the skin of a tomato to break when it is placed in boiling water.

So, when the person next to you gives you the cold shoulder, they are just a cold potato placed in your life to cool you off. However, if you stay hot and close to the source of heat, the potato will either warm or will move out of your way. And who knows, they may be a tomato that has a much shorter cooking time.

Jesus said, the church is to be in the world, and yet not of the world. Sometimes we try to keep the church separate from the world, which is impossible. We cannot live in a community and be daily filled with the Holy Spirit of the living God, without influencing our environment. Call it the spiritual law of physics. Heat will always overcome the cold if the heat remains constant. Everyone was made with the ability to yield to the heat; otherwise, none of us would ever know Him and be changed. In yielding, our spirits are turned to steam and released to move and shake our world in a profound way.

He is the heat, the very energy that created life in the beginning, and when we yield to Him, we too become vessels of the heat. However, if we try to keep our spiritual lives separate, we will be stuck in the cold stew of the world where we can't move, much less make a difference. When the source of heat is removed, the cooling process instantly begins again. The spirit of the living God is the heat, the ingredient that must be present to release the liquid and set us free.

Your prayers affect the heat flow in and through your life. You can make a difference as you pray and remain constantly connected to the source of heat. You are the steam that is released to move and shake the *stew pot* of your community so it too, becomes warm.

Prayer

Oh Lord use me to change the world around me. Fill me with your hot holy fire. Give me courage to make a difference in my community.

Reflections

What stands out to you in the story?

_____

_____

_____

_____

What is God speaking to your heart through this life
lesson?

_____

_____

_____

_____

My Journal

_____

_____

_____

_____

_____

A Butterfly Takes Flight

First Baptism

The Lord protects those of childlike faith;
I was facing death, and he saved me.

Psalm 116:6, NLT

Life Lesson

Our salvation from sin and the promise of eternal life in Heaven are secured by Jesus' death on the cross and the blood He shed. All we need to be saved is child-like faith that accepts Jesus as savior, yet sometimes children who accept Jesus as savior, don't really understand what they are praying.

What I learned from my own experience, is that parents need to clearly explain salvation through the lens of God's grace and mercy. This will help children understand who God is and how deeply He loves us.

****

I was a very uncomfortable four-year-old, as I sat with my family in church. The pews were hard, and we had to sit still. If you wiggled or made any noise you would get a thump on the head, which really hurt. I would try to think of fun things to occupy my time while I waited for the very, very long, and boring service to close. I thought of a pleasant trip where I got to get ice cream.

Recently, we had visited my mother's family in her hometown. Her brother owned the City Café and took me, without my brother, to the Café and gave me an ice cream cone. It was usually my brother who got to go places while I had to stay at home, so to be selected to go was wonderful. I don't remember where my brother was, but knew I was the only one who got to go with my Uncle Richard that day. So, during the long boring part of the service I was remembering how great it was to be the one chosen to go with Uncle Richard for ice cream. He instantly became my favorite of my mother's four brothers.

After we got home, I was still thinking about Uncle Richard and wanted to tell my mother, who was cooking lunch.

I went in the kitchen and said, "Guess what I was thinking during the sermon this morning."

Mother shut off the fire on the stove, took me by the hand and led me into the dining room where she sat down, took me on her lap and asked, "What were you thinking, Norene?"

I knew she expected me to say something *churchie* and I didn't want to disappoint her, so I said "God," in the most solemn voice I could muster.

Well Mother immediately asked me if I wanted to go to the front and talk to the pastor. The fat was in the fire now for sure, because that was the last thing I wanted. I don't know why I didn't tell my mother the truth. It simply never occurred to me. She asked me every day if I wanted to go talk to the pastor, and every Sunday when the invitation was given, she insisted I go talk to the Pastor.

One Sunday, I don't remember how it happened, because I know I didn't want to go talk to the Pastor, but Mother took me anyway. The Pastor asked me some questions and I must have answered correctly because he said they were having an evening baptismal service, and that we should come back to church for it.

In my short life, I had no memory of ever seeing a baptismal service, but no one in my family thought about that, so they didn't prepare me for what was coming. Mother left me in this little room by myself with the Pastor. He called me to come to him. He got into this tank of water, lifted me in beside him and had me stand on a stool, so my head was not under water.

The next thing I knew he had a handkerchief over my face and nose and pushed my head under the water. I was terrified. I thought he was trying to drown me and started kicking and hitting. It was not a good experience.

At age twelve, when I was old enough to understand I needed a Savior, the memory of this baptism created a struggle for me. During church services, when they gave the invitation for people who wanted to have a personal relationship with Jesus to come forward, I would tell myself I had already been baptized, so I didn't need to do anything else. I thought if I just quit sinning, I would be fine because I had been baptized already.

We went to church Sunday morning and night, and again on Wednesday night for a prayer service. I disliked Wednesday night the most. One particular Wednesday I decided to fake a headache to see if I could stay home. It worked. I had the whole evening to myself, which didn't happen often in our house. I made sure I was in bed before the family got home from church.

I was afraid to go to sleep. I vowed I wouldn't sin anymore and yet I lied to my parents, so I thought if I died that night I would go straight to hell.

Finally, I recognized that I knew how to be saved. Our little country Baptist Church was big on that teaching. So, as I lay in bed I prayed and asked Jesus to come into my heart so I wouldn't go to hell, and then waited. Peace and joy came to me and the fear of death disappeared. Jesus saved me! Despite my trauma as a four-year-old, I have walked with Jesus since I was twelve years old.

Prayer

Thank you, Lord for placing me in a Christian home where I could learn about You, even when I didn't understand You. Thank you for giving Your life for mine, as a substitution for my sin. Thank you, Jesus, for saving me.

Reflections

What stands out to you in the story?

_____

_____

_____

_____

What is God speaking to your heart through this life
lesson?

_____

_____

_____

_____

My Journal

_____

_____

_____

_____

_____

Thank God for Blue Jays

Son of man, I have made you a watchman for the house of Israel; therefore, hear a word from My mouth, and give them warning from Me:

Ezekiel 3:17, NIV

Life Lesson

The Lord has taught me to heed warnings from church leaders in certain times. He speaks to the prophets to guide us, and we have wise prophets even in this modern day. God warns us through the prophets and others around us, because He wants to save us from harm.

****

Early one summer morning I sat in my backyard talking to God, listening to the twitter of birds and watching the day awake. A blue jay startled the calm with a scolding irritating voice that grated on my nerves.

I asked God, "Why did you put an irritating voice in such a beautiful creature?"

To my surprise, He answered, "Watch, you'll understand."

I finally saw the bird diving then flying, only to dive again. As I kept watch in the dim light, I saw a white cat slowly creeping along the ground. It was beautiful with white fluffy fur and innocent blue eyes. What was he stalking? At first, I couldn't see what the cat was after when a movement caught my eye. A defenseless little brown bird was just feet away.

The jay's insistent warning and threatening dive bombing continued with relentless will.

I thought, "Oh, little bird, hear the blue jay's warning."

The enemy, beautiful but intent upon evil, only ignored the jay's protest and attack. The little bird finally heeded the bluebird's cry and flew to the safety of his nest in a nearby tree.

The cat did not quit or relax his posture but approached the tree and began to climb the trunk. I leapt to my feet prepared to run to the rescue of the helpless little bird.

I thought, "No, he would not be the cat's breakfast!"

Before I could take a step, an amazing thing happened. To my untrained ear there was no noticeable difference in the blue jay's call. But, as if awaiting a signal from their commander, a squadron of jays arrived in formation and started to attack in earnest. One after another, in perfect rhythm, they pecked white fur from the tail, back, head and even ears of the enemy cat who was by now halfway up the tree trunk.

I compare this to the warnings we receive from those around us in the Body of Christ. How often do we ignore the prophet's warning, thinking "I can handle it," or not recognize the danger that looks so pretty and fun? We are so easily deceived.

At a decided disadvantage, the cat halted his pursuit, unable to defend himself while climbing. A small brown bird breakfast was not worth the price after all. He retreated in defeat. Instantly the blue jays stopped their tirade and disappeared as quickly as they came.

In the sudden silence, I pondered the role the blue jays play in the bird world. They are like prophets. I remembered some *blue jays* in my own life who gave me warnings I didn't want to hear. I didn't want to listen to their warning cries. Their voices grated on my serene and self-controlled world. Now I know that God sends these warnings because He wants to keep me from harm.

Prayer

Oh God, let me heed the blue jay's warning, warning against seemingly harmless and innocent things that are as destructive to me as an attack cat is to a little bird. Thank you, God, for blue jays and their warning cries.

Reflections

What stands out to you in the story?

_____

_____

_____

_____

What is God speaking to your heart through this life
lesson?

_____

_____

_____

_____

My Journal

_____

_____

_____

_____

_____

Mary and Martha

And she had a sister called Mary, who also sat at Jesus'
feet and heard His word. But Martha was distracted with
much serving, and she approached Him and said, "Lord,
do You not care that my sister has left me to serve alone?
Therefore tell her to help me."
And Jesus answered and said to her, "Martha, Martha, you
are worried and troubled about many things. But one thing
is needed, and Mary has chosen that good part, which will
not be taken away from her.

Luke 10:39-42, NKJV

Life Lesson

Many times, in my life I was so busy serving others
that I became resentful. God showed me this so I could see
that the point of serving people is not to stay busy and look
good, but to serve them with the love and grace of Jesus.
Sitting at His feet and worshipping Him is far more
important than staying busy doing for Him.

****

It was the Memorial Day Weekend Church Camping Trip, and I served as the chief cook and bottle washer for several younger singles, who I organized to pool resources and share food. This Monday morning, I woke up tired and sore. I was full of resentment toward the people I served and was probably the only person in camp not having fun. I needed an attitude adjustment.

I walked to the woods to be alone with the Lord. As I muttered along with no thought for direction, my feet took me to the highest point on the grounds to a large wooden cross. I worked through the first rush of resentment and anger during my tramp through the woods and the push up the hill, so I sat down at the foot of the cross to rest and cool off.

My churning, angry heart and mind stilled for the first time as I viewed the peaceful beauty surrounding me. On the back side of this high hill, I noticed woods and trails, and little clearings with altars tucked at random among the acres of trees. From the front side of this hill, I surveyed the spectacular valley with a river-bend at the bottom, lush green pastures sprinkled with daises and buttercups and other unidentified beauties. The blue of the water, the bright clean sky, the warm sun, the contrasting pleasant cool breeze, the broad expanse of valley, all were at my feet. I delighted in two young colts playing tag then racing back to the haven of their mom's side, only to dart off again. Four or five other horses grazed methodically. The soft breeze felt good as it blew on my hot face. The only sound I heard was the swish of the tall prairie grass as it rippled and swayed in the wind.

My anger and resentment melted away and the Lord's peace covered me as I sat at the foot of the cross. I repented and thought about the awesome world God created. He gave me the opportunity to sit here to enjoy and receive his refreshment.

I nearly missed it simply by focusing on my frustrations. I chose to fret, stew and focus on the work, never resting even when the work was finished. All I could see was how much I did and what I had to do next. I realized I was acting like Martha in the story where Jesus visited Mary and Martha at their home. Mary sat at Jesus' feet listening to His wisdom, while Martha scurried around and even asked the Lord, why He didn't make Mary help her with all the work.

I acknowledged and repented of all the resentment I harbored in my heart. I carefully planned each meal but failed to plan for help in meal preparation. I didn't plan time for the Lord or for me. I realized that I expected someone to notice that I needed help and offer it. I was too proud to ask. Also, a part of me wanted to do it all by myself so I would be appreciated for all the work I was doing.

I thought, "Yuck! That's stinking thinking!"

Then I prayed, "Lord I also repent of pride and trying to get my significance from others, from looking for affirmation from people instead of from You. This keeps me from serving with a sincere heart."

I knelt at the foot of the cross and continued to pray, "Oh Lord, forgive me for ignoring You and the magnificence of your creation. Teach me to see all there is to see. Let me never again miss You and what You have for me because I'm too busy to stop and notice You. I want to experience all there is to experience, to see everything there is to see. I don't want to look back on my life to see a deep rut made by the drudgery of work; never growing; never experiencing life. Oh God, change my heart and adjust my eyes so I never again miss what you have for me to see, or what You want to teach me. Teach me to look for you in everything around me. Teach me your truth that is demonstrated and revealed in all of creation."

I thought about the scripture in Romans that refers to how clearly we can see God's majesty through His beautiful creation.

They know the truth about God because He has made it obvious to them. For ever since the world was created, people have seen the earth and sky. Through everything God made, they can clearly see His invisible qualities – His eternal power and divine nature, so they have no excuse for not knowing God.

Romans 1:19-20, NLT

Prayer

Forgive me Father for serving with a resentful heart. I have so much to be grateful for. You are a wonderful and good God and have created a majestic, beautiful planet for me to enjoy. Thank you for reminding me to be a cheerful giver.

Reflections

What stands out to you in the story?

_____

_____

_____

_____

What is God speaking to your heart through this life lesson?

_____

_____

_____

_____

My Journal

_____

_____

_____

_____

_____

The Railroad Track

The Lord himself goes before you and will be with you; he will never leave you nor forsake you. Do not be afraid; do not be discouraged.

Deuteronomy 31:8, NIV

Life Lesson

As a single mom with two children, sometimes at church, I was left out. These were painful experiences, but the Lord showed me that I needed to stay on track with Him. When I focus on Him and following where He is leading me, I can walk through anything, even rejection, in a place where I expect total acceptance.

****

One Sunday evening, I took a walk right before sunset along the railroad track running near my house. As I walked along watching the rail, I had a vision of the track flexing and straightening as the wheels of a train went across the track.

The Lord said to me, "That is like a Christian; strong as steel but flexible so as not to break when carrying a heavy load."

I continued to walk and meditate on how a Christian could be like a railroad track. To me an obvious feature was how the bedrock under the rails represented Jesus, who is called the rock of our salvation.

I was stepping from railroad tie to railroad tie so asked Jesus, "If the rails represent a Christian's life and the hard bedrock underneath is Jesus, what do these ties represent?"

The instant answer was almost overwhelming. "They are the family, friends, teachers and pastors, who I have placed in your life to support you."

I stopped and looked back and as far as I could see there were railroad ties every two or three feet. I turned and in front of me I could see the setting sun reflected on the shiny track as it disappeared into the sun itself. And again, every two or three feet there was another railroad tie. God brought to my mind old memories of pleasant and not so pleasant times and the people who were there to share both my joys and sorrows.

I stood for a long time meditating on how this could be. I felt the love of God surrounding me as I understood His constant care for me – always. I continued my walk and noticed the loose gravel and rock surrounding the rails and ties.

I asked God, "If this rail is me, and the bedrock is Jesus, and these railroad ties are fellow Christians, what does this loose gravel represent?"

The answer was again immediate as I heard, "It represents the Holy Spirit."

The loose gravel must be continually replenished as the weight of the train causes the track to flex, which moves the rock. Also, the rain can wash it away. Likewise, we need a daily refilling of the Holy Spirit to keep us flexible as we face the trials of each day. The rock is what gives the support and allows the track to bend and yet carry the heavy load. In the same way, the Holy Spirit in our lives is what gives us the needed support to carry the loads we are required to carry.

I was feeling particularly sorry for myself and felt people were taking advantage of me. When I saw a railroad tie almost completely buried in the gravel, God told me that was where I was right then. Someone had leaned on me extra hard because they were too weak to carry their load by themselves. This pushed me closer to the bedrock, Jesus, and was buried in the gravel of the Holy Spirit.

In my mind's eye I saw an abandoned railroad track. The gravel had all been washed away and the track was rusty. The Lord reminded me that sometimes the heavy loads keep us polished and going back to the source to have our daily fill of the rock of the Holy Spirit.

It was getting dark, and I was at the road I needed to take to go home. I took one last look at the track and realized there were two rails and knew the second rail represented Jesus who is our constant companion, the one who is always there to share our load.

I thought, "This is dumb. A railroad track is made to carry a load."

And the answer was immediate, "So is a Christian."

In the next few days as I continued to think on my railroad track experience, I realized God puts as much effort in planning our lives as the engineers who plan and lay a railroad track do. They know exactly how much weight this track will be required to carry, so they know exactly what grade to make the bedrock and the kind of support it will need to withstand the weather and the train loads. And as a track has a beginning and an end, our lives have a beginning and a final destination assured.

I started to meditate on what it means to be a railroad tie and asked God to teach me to be a better support for others. He reminded me what is required to make a railroad tie. It first must be of the right kind of hardwood. Pine or other soft wood could be cut the same shape and size, but the load would crush it. God reminded me there were some soft ties I had chosen in my life; but when I needed them for support, they were not there for me. They were my partying friends. He reminded me a true friend is one who can be trusted through the bad as well as the good times. To be a railroad tie the wood must be soaked in creosote oil to make it usable. This preserves the wood, so it doesn't rot, sprout or get destroyed by insects. In the Bible oil represents the Holy Spirit so we need to be filled, soaked, and totally buried in the Holy Spirit so we are usable in His Kingdom.

A while later a friend suggested I go back to see if God had anything else, He wanted to teach me from the railroad track. As I walked along the track, I noticed there was fresh, deep gravel along the track. Crunching my way through the deep gravel, I saw blotches of occasional orange paint along the inside rail of the track. As I tried to see what this might mean, I realized everywhere there was a blotch of paint there was a new railroad tie.

I asked God what this meant, and He said, "This is a picture of healing of memories." He went on to say, "Things happen in everyone's life when they are hurt by others who have disappointed them or acted mean or cruel. Because you live in a fallen world, sometimes life in general is cruel. And like the railroad track is as strong as the support it has under it; you are as strong in faith as your memories allow you to be."

He asked permission to walk back through my life with me with his paint bucket and place a mark by the old hurts He wanted to heal. Also, there were some current habits I had where I depended on myself instead of allowing Him to provide the answers. He wanted me to let Him replace my own strength with His more perfect will and strength to meet my every need.

This experience set the tone for my relationship with God as I learned to lean on Him.

Prayer

Thank you, Jesus for being my closest companion, walking with me through my life, supporting and loving me.

Reflections

What stands out to you in the story?

_____

_____

_____

_____

What is God speaking to your heart through this life lesson?

_____

_____

_____

_____

My Journal

_____

_____

_____

_____

The Garden of My Heart

*Therefor be imitators of God as dear children. And walk in
love, as Christ also has loved us and given Himself for us,
an offering and a sacrifice to God for a sweet-smelling
aroma.*

*For you were once darkness, but now you are light in the
Lord. Walk as children of light.*

Ephesians 5:1-2, 8, NKJV

Life Lesson

Through my years of seeking to have an intimate
relationship with God, I've found that dwelling in His
presence is an all-encompassing part of my walk with Him.
Sitting in His presence brings peace, joy and revelation.
I'm overwhelmed to know that a magnificent and mighty

God wants me to experience Him in such a way, that I am drawn into His heavenly realm.

****

The first time I encountered God in my secret heart garden was in a class titled, *The Presence of God.* We were instructed to close our eyes and let Jesus show us the garden of our hearts.

All I could see was one huge tree. It was so big it was hard for the light to penetrate. Its shadow created so much darkness that nothing else could grow. The session leader prayed for me and named the tree *fear*. I repented of giving fear a place in my life and watched as Jesus lifted the tree and tossed it into outer space, slinging it like a spear.

Later, when I went to Morton Arboretum in Wheaton, Illinois, I experienced another trip to my heart garden. This arboretum is at the home of the man who founded the Morton Salt Company. He was interested in trees so he brought trees and plants from everywhere back to the Chicago area, to see which ones would grow well there. The garden is now open to the public and is beautiful.

I packed a sandwich, bottle of water, my Bible, and my prayer journal in my backpack and spent most of the day hiking and talking out loud to the Lord. When I first got there, I kept running into people. People were everywhere and I wanted to be alone with God.

I was complaining to the Lord about all the people, and He said, "Mankind is my greatest possession."

I answered, "I know, but there are too many people in the park today for me to enjoy being alone with You."

Again, He said, "Mankind is my greatest possession."

I felt His sadness when I was unable to enjoy other people being around and realized I needed an attitude adjustment. He cared as much for each of them as He did for me. I repented for my bad attitude and continued walking. I have this internal drive that makes it difficult for me not to see what is over the next hill, so found myself wandering along every path. Apparently, I took the *path less traveled* as I found myself going under a road to the other side of the park, where there were few people. I was more comfortable walking and talking aloud to the Lord where no one could hear me. The path I was on passed a small flower plot called the Fragrance Garden. I stopped to smell the wonderful fragrances but there was one smell that seemed to linger in my nose. I walked away but kept remembering the smell, so went back. I found a small sprig of dried flowers on the bottom part of the plant, so I broke it off and carried it with me, sniffing it occasionally.

Off the path a little way I noticed a high metal fence surrounding a plot of ground that was so overgrown I couldn't see into it. I left the path and had to climb a hill to find what it was. I walked around the fence, trying to find an entrance, also trying to see what it contained. I found a gate with a large padlock on it but was never able to see inside the overgrown space. I suspected it was the family burial plot but was not sure. I sat on the ground by the tree a few yards from the fence to rest.

I considered climbing the fence to see what it was when the Lord said, "Ask me why the fence and locked gate are there."

So, I asked Him, "Why is the fence there and why is it locked?"

He answered, "This place is considered holy, so they have locked it to protect it."

I remembered the garden in my heart from before and asked, "Lord is there a locked garden inside my heart?"

He answered, "The fenced place in your heart is a burial ground and the fragrance you picked is anointing for burial. Are you ready to die?"

I thought on this for a long time but concluded I must go on with the Lord. I was unwilling to stay where I was; I wanted and needed to be able to open my heart to the Lord so if He required me to die, so be it.

The Lord continued, "When you feel self-pity, you indulge yourself with compulsive eating or other ways to make you feel good. This is a place within you that is a place of death; a place where Jesus is not. He can't come there because it is a place of sin."

Now, I chose to open the lock so Jesus could come into this place of my garden heart. He waited for me to unlock the gate and invite Him in. I was going to tear down the fence and tear off the gate when Jesus reached out His hand and stopped me.

He said, "This is still a private holy place for you to meet with Me, our private garden." He wanted it to remain locked to others.

As Jesus and I walked into the garden it was choked with vines growing on the ground and climbing all the fences. I knew it was self-pity and self-indulgence, so repented of giving into these sins. It was choking the life and light out of the garden. I set off walking briskly through the garden, pulling handfuls of vines to quickly get rid of them, when I realized Jesus wasn't with me. I stopped, looked back, and saw Him kneeling by the gate working with his hands in the soil. I walked back and asked Him what he was doing.

He said, "I am planting praise."

I asked, "What does praise look like to you, Lord?"

He said, "Fragrant as the fragrance garden and more beautiful than you have ever seen. Just as this fenced garden is large, overgrown and dark, so is your heart and we are not going to hurry through it. This replanting and reclaiming will take time and cooperation. As the weeds in your garden heart are discovered, they need to be named, repented of, then pulled out and replaced by praise. It didn't get this overgrown overnight so it will take time to reclaim the territory. Now go back to the path of Joy; it is going to rain."

As I left the private garden, I saw a sign, and the path I had been following was called Joy Path. Apparently, it was named for one of the children, Joy Morton. Before I got to the car it began to sprinkle; however, the Lord's instruction to go back to the path of Joy, and the coming rain had a much more significant meaning to me.

I was so grateful for all the Lord had shown me, especially since we had our own garden, our secret place. Here I could be intimate with Him and share all my heart. I had the freedom to speak with Him openly and repent for allowing sin to take space in my heart. Beyond that, I could joyfully and freely praise Him with all my heart! The fragrance of His love that flowed to and through me made such an impact! Oh, to spend time with Him in our garden! All I could do was praise Him, as the only thing I could give Him was praise for all He had done.

Prayer

Thank you, Lord, for meeting with me in our secret place. I do repent of allowing any sin to take space in my heart. I so long to meet with you in the beautiful, fragrant garden we have established in my heart. Help me make praise and meeting with you the top priority in my life.

Reflections

What stands out to you in the story?

_____

_____

_____

_____

What is God speaking to your heart through this life
lesson?

_____

_____

_____

_____

My Journal

_____

_____

_____

_____

_____

Epilogue

As I reviewed each of the chapters for this book, I was surprised at the fact that over and over God helped me with the same issues in my life at different levels.

These themes include:

- Fear
- Poor self-image
- Trauma
- Independent, Self-reliant, Know-it-all
- Anger
- Lack of faith

Some of these traits helped me navigate my life, yet in some cases they got in the way of my walk with Christ. In spite of all my humanness, God continued to pursue me, talk to me, take care of me, love me. I pray in some way my story encourages you to pursue Jesus and learn to receive His love. Learn to see His hand in the very nature around you.